3 0116 01395273 2

WE COME FROM

ROYAL BO

This b
Adult
The
requ

Nigeria

ALISON BROWNLIE

HODDER
Wayland

an imprint of Hodder Children's Books

WE COME FROM

Brazil • China • France
Germany • India • Jamaica • Japan
Kenya • Nigeria • South Africa

The family you are about to meet lives in a city called Lagos. Like any country, Nigeria has many different types of lifestyle. People live in the countryside, as well as in towns and cities.

Cover: Morning assembly in a primary school near Lagos.
Title page (top to bottom): A busy street in Lagos; a farm in the countryside; the central mosque in Abuja; a man climbs a tree to pick coconuts; a girl selling bread in the market in Lagos.
Contents page: Two Nigerian boys.
Index: Nnedima and her cousins in their best clothes, ready to go to church.

All Wayland books encourage children to read and help them improve their literacy.

✓ The contents page, page numbers, headings and index help locate specific pieces of information.

✓ The glossary reinforces alphabetic knowledge and extends vocabulary.

✓ The further information section suggests other books dealing with the same subject.

KENSINGTON & CHELSEA
LIBRARIES SERVICE

513046	
000633	
PETERS	J966.905
N	

First published in Great Britain in 1999 by Wayland Publishers Ltd
This paperback edition published in 2002 by Hodder Wayland,
an imprint of Hodder Children's Books

© Hodder Wayland 1999

Hodder Children's Books
A division of Hodder Headline Limited
338 Euston Road, London NW1 3BH

British Library Cataloguing in Publication Data
Brownlie, Alison, 1949–
 We come from Nigeria
 1. Nigeria – Geography – Juvenile literature
 2. Nigeria – Social conditions – 1960 – Juvenile literature
 I. Title II. Nigeria
 966.9'053

ISBN 0 7502 4387 2

Typeset by Jean Wheeler, England
Printed and bound in Hong Kong

Editor: Alison Cooper
Series editors: Katie Orchard & Polly Goodman
Designer: Jean Wheeler
Production controller: Tracy Fewtrell

Picture Acknowledgements: Associated Press/Topham 9; Axiom *contents page*, 20 (bottom)/James Morris, 22/James Morris, 29 (top right)/Guy Marks; Hutchison 19 (bottom)/ Juliet Highet, 20 (top)/Anna Tully; Panos *Cover*, 21/Betty Press; Still Pictures 23/Mark Edwards; Wayland Picture Library 6, 7(top), 8 (bottom)/James Morris, 26 (top); Morounke Williams *title page* (second from bottom), 8 (top). All the other photographs are by Pierre Chuckwudi Alozie. The map on page 5 is by Peter Bull.

Contents

Welcome to Nigeria! 4

Land and Weather 6

At Home 10

Nigerian Food 14

At Work 18

At School 20

Free Time 24

Looking Ahead 26

Hide-and-seek 28

Nigeria Fact File 29

Topic Web 30

Extension Activities 30

Glossary 31

Further Information 31

Index 32

Welcome to Nigeria!

'My name is Nnedima. In this photo I'm wearing my best pink dress for church.'

Nnedima ▶ *(pronounced 'Ned-im-a') with her aunt and four of her cousins.*

Nnedima is eleven years old. She lives in Ikeja, a suburb of the city of Lagos. You can see where Lagos is on the map on page 5. Nnedima's parents live far away in Umuahia, a village in eastern Nigeria. Nnedima lives with her aunt, uncle and cousins.

*▼ Nigeria is a very big country.
A quarter of all Africans live there.*

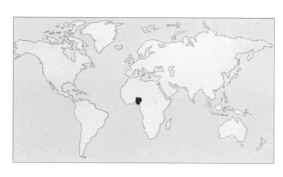

▲ Nigeria's place in the world.

0	100	200 miles
0	100 200	300 km

NIGERIA

Capital city	Abuja
Land area	923,768 square kilometres
Population	104 million people (1996 estimate)
Main languages	English (official), Hausa, Ibo and Yoruba
Main religions	Islam in the north, Christianity in the south

5

Land and Weather

Most of Nigeria is flat. There are some low mountains in the east and around the centre of the country.

A hot, dry wind from the Sahara desert blows across northern Nigeria. There is little rain, so only a few trees grow on the grassy plains.

▼ *The Jos Plateau in central Nigeria.*

▲ *The Seven Stream waterfall in southern Nigeria.*

As you travel south, the land becomes greener. At certain times of the year there is a lot of rain here, so more trees and plants are able to grow.

▶ *The roads are sometimes damaged by floods in the rainy season.*

Thick rain forest grows in southern Nigeria. Along the coast there are sandy beaches and areas of very wet land, called swamps.

Plants called mangroves grow in the swamps. Their tangled roots grow high above the ground.

▲ *The coast is lined with palm trees.*

▼ *Heavy rain helps the rain forest to grow.*

'Lagos is the biggest city in Nigeria.' Nnedima.

Many of the towns and cities are in the south. Lagos, where Nnedima lives, is a busy port. Most of the city is built on an island.

At Home

Most Nigerians live in the countryside, in houses made from blocks of earth. A child's parents, grandparents, aunts and uncles usually live together in a compound. A compound is a group of small houses, built around a central yard.

▲ *A woman washes clothes and hangs them up to dry.*

▼ *Houses made from earth stay cool in the heat of the day.*

▶ *A quarter of all Nigerians live in the towns and cities.*

11

▲ *Nnedima's aunt does some chores in the yard.*

Nnedima lives in Lagos with her aunt and uncle so that she can go to school. She also helps her aunt to look after the younger children.

Nnedima shares a bedroom with one of her cousins. There are two other bedrooms, a living room, a kitchen and a bathroom in her uncle's flat.

▶ *Nnedima's aunt and cousins in their living room.*

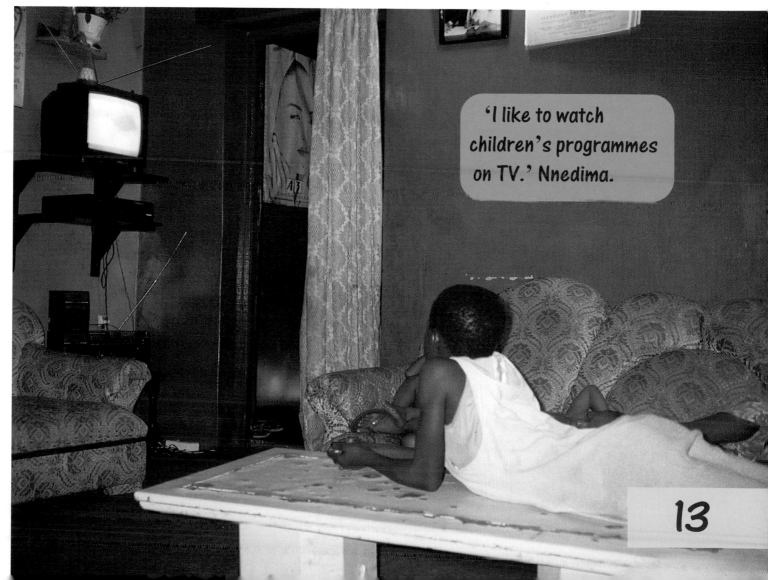

'I like to watch children's programmes on TV.' Nnedima.

Nigerian Food

Nigerians are able to grow most of the food they need in their own country. Yams are an important food. A yam is a vegetable like a potato, which can be boiled, roasted or pounded.

▶ *These farmers are preparing the ground so that they can plant yams.*

▼ *Piles of yams on sale in the market in Lagos.*

14

Nigerians like spicy, peppery food.
They enjoy soups and stews made
from vegetables, beans and fish.

In the villages people usually grow their own food. But Nnedima's aunt has to go to the market every day to buy fresh vegetables, meat and fish. Sometimes Nnedima goes to the market to get bread.

◀ *Nnedima's cousin slices vegetables, ready to make soup.*

16

'I help my aunt by washing the vegetables for dinner.' Nnedima.

At Work

In the countryside, most people are farmers. They grow rice, maize, yams and cassavas, and they keep chickens and goats. In the north many people herd sheep and goats. They move from place to place, looking for fresh pasture for their animals.

▼ *At markets, farmers sell the food that their own families do not need.*

18

Many young people move to the cities to look for work. They may get jobs in offices, factories, or stores.

▲ *A tailor making clothes in Lagos*

▼ *Women at work in a busy bank in Lagos*

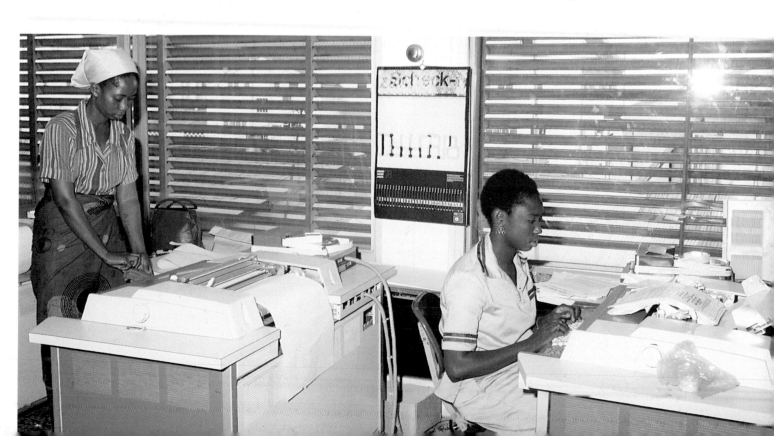

At School

Until a few years ago, children used to learn from the older people in their villages. Now most children go to school to learn.

▶ *Classes often have more than forty pupils.*

'My favourite subject is English.' Nnedima.

The school day starts early, at eight o'clock in the morning. Most children go home for lunch. School usually finishes by two o'clock because it is too hot to work in the afternoon.

▲ *Sometimes classes take place outside.*

All Nnedima's lessons are in English, but at home she often speaks Ibo with her relatives. At school she learns about the history and geography of Nigeria, as well as doing maths, science and sports.

▶ *Most children walk home from school.*

▼ *School children playing outside their school.*

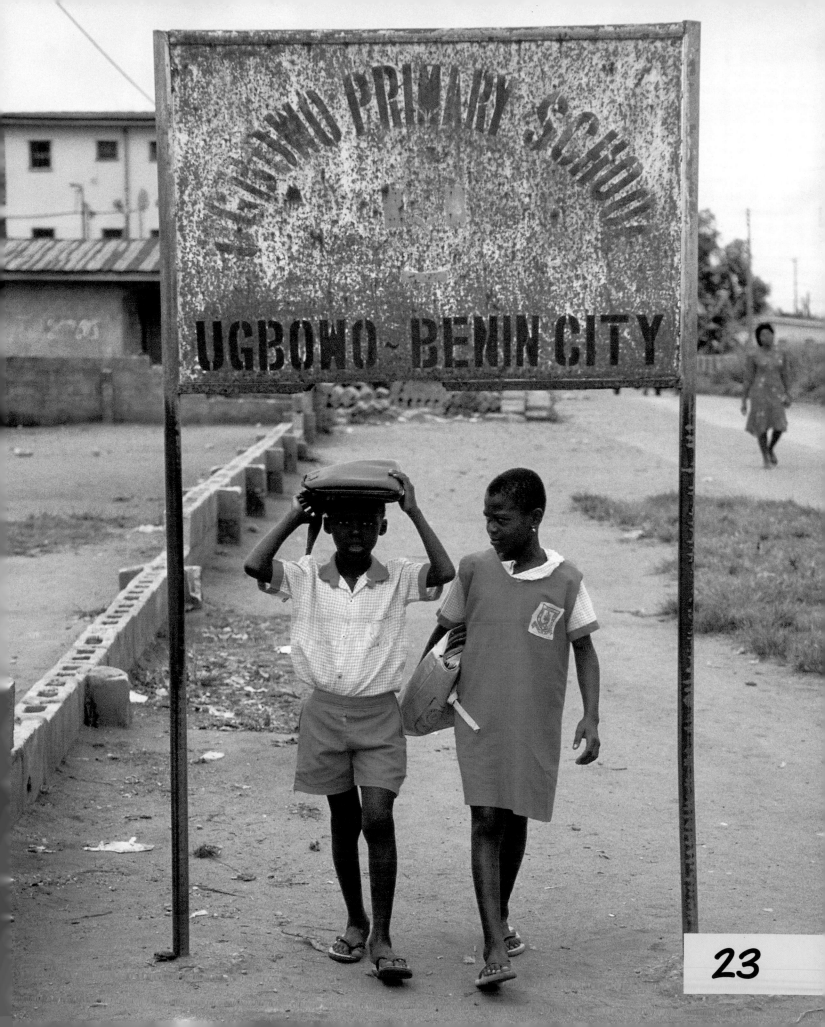

Free Time

People in Nigeria enjoy many festivals. At celebrations such as naming ceremonies and weddings there is a lot of singing and dancing.

People who live in the towns and cities can go to the cinema or a funfair, or they can visit a museum.

▲ The whole family enjoys a visit to the museum.

◀ These teenagers in Lagos are having a pedalo race.

Looking Ahead

In the last few years, Nigeria has been ruled by a dictator. Many people would like to be able to choose a new leader.

There is a lot of oil in Nigeria. Nigerians hope that their country will get more money from selling the oil in the future. Then they might be able to build better roads, schools and hospitals.

▲ *Many Nigerians work in the oil industry.*

▼ *Abuja has been the capital of Nigeria since 1991.*

Hide-and-seek

Nnedima likes to play hide-and-seek with her cousins and her friends from the flat upstairs. In Nigeria hide-and-seek is called *b'oju b'oju*.

To play hide-and-seek, close your eyes and count to 100. While you are doing this, all your friends must find somewhere to hide.

▲ *Nnedima with her cousins and friends.*

When you have counted to 100, open your eyes and see how quickly you can find your friends.

Nnedima usually finds her friends quite quickly but her cousin Ichioma is very good at finding places to hide. It takes Nnedima a long while to find her.

◀ *Nnedima and her friends run off to hide.*

Nigeria Fact File

◀ Money facts

Nigeria's money is the naira. There are 100 kobo in 1 naira. £1 is worth about 55 naira.

▼ Population

Nigeria has the largest population in Africa. The population is made up of over 250 ethnic groups. The largest groups are the Fulani, the Hausa, the Yoruba and the Ibo. Each group has its own customs; many groups have their own language, too.

▶ Benin bronzes

This is one of the famous Benin bronzes. Most of these beautiful figures were made in Nigeria about 300 years ago.

Independence Day

Nigeria was ruled by Britain for many years but it became independent on 1 October 1960. October 1st is now a national holiday.

▼ The Nigerian flag

The colours in the Nigerian flag have special meanings. The green represents farming and the richness of the land. The white represents peace.

Football

Football is the most popular sport in Nigeria. The national team, the Super Eagles, got through to the final rounds of the 1998 World Cup.

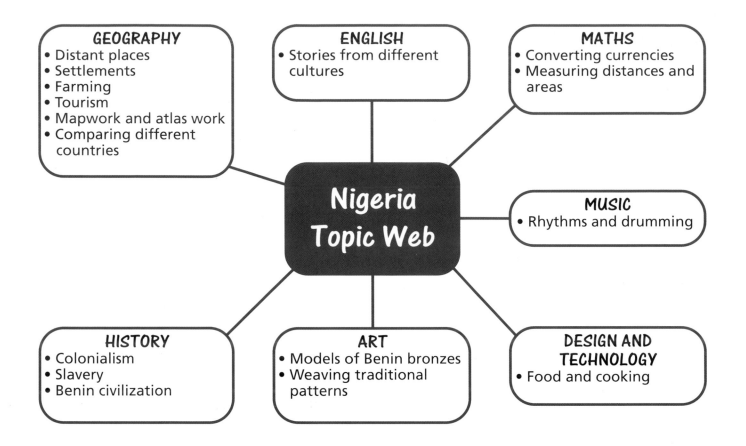

GEOGRAPHY
- Distant places
- Settlements
- Farming
- Tourism
- Mapwork and atlas work
- Comparing different countries

ENGLISH
- Stories from different cultures

MATHS
- Converting currencies
- Measuring distances and areas

Nigeria Topic Web

MUSIC
- Rhythms and drumming

HISTORY
- Colonialism
- Slavery
- Benin civilization

ART
- Models of Benin bronzes
- Weaving traditional patterns

DESIGN AND TECHNOLOGY
- Food and cooking

Extension Activities

GEOGRAPHY
- Find Nigeria in an atlas.
- Work out how many times the UK would fit into Nigeria.
- Ask the children to make a list of all the similarities between their lives and Nnedima's.

ENGLISH
- Ask the children to imagine they are on holiday in Nigeria. What would they write on a postcard home? What is Nigeria like?
- Read a story from Nigeria (see suggestions in list of further reading).

ART
- Find out about Nigerian weaving.
- Make your own designs based on Nigerian patterns.

MUSIC
- Listen to music from Nigeria.
- Find out about the instruments used to make traditional music.

INFORMATION TECHNOLOGY
- Find out more information about Nigeria from the Internet.

Glossary

Desert A very dry area of land, where only a few plants and animals can survive.

Dictator Someone who takes command of a country without having been chosen by the people.

Ethnic group A group of people who share the same language and customs.

Mosque A place where Muslims go to pray and hold religious ceremonies.

Naming ceremony A ceremony at which a baby is given its name.

Pedalo A small boat that has pedals to make it move.

Plains Areas of flat land.

Plateau An area of high, fairly flat land.

Rain forest Thick forest that grows in places where the weather is hot and very wet all year round.

Suburb An area of a town or city where people live, away from the centre.

Further Information

Fiction:

A is for Africa by Ifeoma Onyefulu (Frances Lincoln, 1993)

Bitter Bananas by Isaac Olaleye (Boyds Mills Press, 1994)

Emeka's Gift by Ifeoma Onyefulu (Frances Lincoln, 1995)

One Big Family by Ifeoma Onyefulu (Frances Lincoln, 1996)

Non-fiction:

Benin: An African Kingdom by Deborah and Elizabeth Isaacs (International Broadcasting Trust, 1994)

Food and Festivals: A Flavour of West Africa by Alison Brownlie (Wayland, 1998)

Organizations:

Nigerian High Commission, 9 Northumberland Avenue, London WC2 5BX

Index

All the numbers in **bold** refer to illustrations.

Abuja 5, **5**, **26**

Benin bronzes 29, **29**

cities 4, 9, **9**, 11, 19, 24
compound 10, **10**

dictator 26

farmers **14**, 18
festivals 24
flag 29, **29**
food 14–17
  rice and beans 15
  vegetables 14, 15, 16,
  16, **17**
  yams 14, **14**
football 29

hide-and-seek 28, **28**
home life 10–13
houses 10, **10**

Lagos 4, **5**, 9, **9**, 12, 14,
  19, **24**
languages 5, 22

markets **14**, 16, **18**
money 29, **29**
museums 24, **24**

oil 26, **26**

plains 6
population 5, 29

rain 6, 7, **7**, 8
rain forest 8, **8**
religions 5, 25

school 12, 20–23
swamps 8

work 18–19